Let's Read About...
Ruby Bridges

This book is dedicated to
Lucille and Abon Bridges
for having the strength and courage
to take a stand.

—R.B. & G.M.

ISBN 0-439-51362-6
Text copyright © 2003 by Ruby Bridges.
Illustrations copyright © 2003 by Cornelius Van Wright and Ying-Hwa Hu.
All rights reserved. Published by Scholastic Inc.
SCHOLASTIC, CARTWHEEL BOOKS, and associated logos are trademarks and/or registered trademarks of Scholastic Inc.

24 23 22 21 20   9 10 11 12 13 14/0
Printed in the U.S.A.   23
First printing, February 2003

Scholastic
First Biographies

Let's Read About...
Ruby Bridges

by Ruby Bridges
and Grace Maccarone
Illustrated by Cornelius Van Wright
and Ying-Hwa Hu

SCHOLASTIC INC.
New York   Toronto   London   Auckland   Sydney
Mexico City   New Delhi   Hong Kong   Buenos Aires

A long time ago,
some people thought that black people
and white people should not be friends.

In some places,
black people were not allowed
to live in the same neighborhoods
as white people.

In some places,
black people were not allowed
to eat in the same restaurants
as white people.

And in some places,
black children and white children
could not go to the same schools.
This is called segregation.

The United States Government said,
"Segregation is wrong."
People should have a chance
to live where they want,
to eat where they want,
and to go to school where they want.

In 1960,
Ruby Bridges went to kindergarten
in a black school.
She liked her school.
She liked her teacher.
She liked her friends.

But there was a white school
even closer to Ruby's house
than the black school.

The Government said,
"Ruby Bridges should be allowed
to go to the white school."
The school was called
William Frantz Elementary School.

In 1961, Ruby was in first grade.
Ruby's mother took her to the
Frantz School.
Two marshals went with
Ruby and her mother
to make sure that they
would be safe.

Some people did not want Ruby
to go to the white school.
They stood in front of the school
and yelled at Ruby to go away.

The white parents took their children
out of the school.
Ruby was alone with her teacher,
Mrs. Henry.

Ruby loved Mrs. Henry.
And Mrs. Henry loved Ruby.
Ruby was a very good student.
She learned math.
She learned how to read.
Ruby wished the children
would come back.
But they never did.

Then when Ruby was in second grade, the children began to come back to the school.

At last,
Ruby had friends to play with!
Ruby was very, very happy!

Many people read about Ruby
in newspapers and books.

A famous writer, John Steinbeck,
wrote about Ruby.
He wrote that Ruby
was very brave.

Norman Rockwell was an artist
who painted a picture of Ruby.
The painting became very famous.

A First Lady, Eleanor Roosevelt,
wrote a letter to Ruby.
The letter told Ruby
that she was a good American.

Now Ruby is grown-up.
She is married.
She has children.

In 1996, Ruby and Mrs. Henry
were both asked to be
on a TV show.
That was the first time
they had seen each other
in 35 years.
Now they are together again.

Because of Ruby Bridges,
black children and white children
can go to the same schools now.
Ruby likes to visit schools.
She tells her story to children.
She tells children
that black people and white people
can be friends.

She tells children to be kind
to one another.